PRAISE FOR SHYLOCK

"I leapt at the opportunity to present *Shylock* at Vancouver's Shakespeare Festival. It is a fascinating play. Bravo Leiren-Young! Bravo Shylock!"

—*Christopher Gaze, Artistic Director*
Bard on the Beach Theatre Company

"*Shylock* is an amazing play and what's amazing about it is that it touches so many important issues in our society about stereotypes and artistic integrity that are especially resonant for non-profit theaters. It's also extraordinarily funny."

—*Bernard Havard, Artistic Director,*
Walnut Street Theatre

"Now that Mark Leiren-Young has done it, we can be surprised that no one thought before of dramatizing the conflict caused by Shylock today."

—*Mavor Moore*

"This is good storytelling that makes great theatre."
—*Peter C. Newman*

"An engrossing monologue . . . while playwright Leiren-Young makes it clear what he thinks about the issues surrounding *The Merchant of Venice*, he presents the controversy about its performance and censorship fully and fairly. *Shylock* is a provocative play that gets you thinking."

—*Douglas Keating, The Philadelphia Inquirer*

SHYLOCK

a play

by

Mark Leiren-Young

ANVIL PERFORMANCE SERIES

Printed and bound in Canada
2nd Edition, Revised & Enlarged
(2nd Printing: November, 2001)
Cover Design: Rayola Graphic Design
Cover photo of William Leach by Coy Butler

Canadian Cataloguing in Publication Data

Leiren-Young, Mark, 1962-
Shylock

ISBN 1-895636-12-4

1. Title
PS8573.E478S59 1996   C812'.54   C96-910512-6
PR9199.3.L42S59 1996

Represented in Canada by the Literary Press Group
Distributed by General Distribution Services

The publisher gratefully acknowledges the assistance of the B.C. Arts Council, the Canada Council for the Arts and the Book Publishing Industry Development Program (BPIDP) for their support of our publishing program.

The Canada Council | Le Conseil des Arts
for the Arts | du Canada

BRITISH
COLUMBIA
ARTS COUNCIL
Supported by the Province of British Columbia

Anvil Press
Suite 204-A 175 East Broadway,
Vancouver, BC V5T 1W2 CANADA
www.anvilpress.com

Contents

Acknowledgements

S*hylock* was originally published just a few days before it first appeared on stage in Vancouver, Canada and, since then, the list of people who deserve thanks for bringing this play to life has grown to the point where I could fill another book with their names.

My first thank you is to all the directors, artistic directors, designers, stage managers, technicians and everyone else involved with the various productions—especially all the actors who devoted themselves to becoming Jon Davies.

And now, in something resembling chronological order . . .

Thanks to . . . William Shakespeare for the use of his words; Bard on the Beach and Christopher Gaze for allowing *Shylock* to be the first work not written by Shakespeare to appear under their tent; David Berner for having the chutzpah to be the first actor to play Jon Davies; Errol Durbach for his thoughtful essay; Patrick Stewart for his encouragement (yes, that Patrick Stewart); Brian Kaufman and Anvil Press for believing in the script; John Juliani and Donna Wong-Juliani for their passion, devotion and friendship, and Joan Watterson for her work as a dramaturge and unofficial agent which led directly to . . .

The Walnut Street Theatre, Bernard Havard and Deborah Bloch, who directed the Philadelphia production, and prompted a lot of the fine tuning that has taken place between the first edition of the script and this one.

Thanks to Ken Smedley and the George Ryga Centre for mounting a production with John Huston, who made audiences believe that a Métis actor in his early-thirties was a Jewish man in his forties; Ian Ferguson, Paul Soles and Jan Lewis for their faith in the play and the San Diego Repertory Theatre, Tod Salovey and Ron Campbell for bringing this to the Jewish Arts Festival in San Diego.

On a personal note, thanks to Steve Kaplan for getting me into theatre in the first place; Gary Poole, Juliana Saxton, Art Norris and Bob Hogg for believing; Lise Magee and Gordon Miller for their friendship; Hall and Carol Leiren, David, Cindy and Emma Young for their love; my Zaida Ben Wosk for everything, and especially Darron Leiren-Young for her love, support and willingness to put up with all the voices and worlds in my head.

—*MLY, September 2001*

Introduction

An introduction to a script is a bit like a rock video for a song. It can stop the reader from using their own imagination and creating their own images and interpretations. Some writers may like this idea but I'm not convinced that playwrights can ever completely know what their work is "about," just what they intended when they created it.

When I first set out to write *Shylock* I wanted to create a play about censorship. The issue has always fascinated me and I was looking for a way to explore it on stage.

I'd been working on a historical drama about an event that took place in Canada just after World War One, but I was frustrated because I wasn't sure that a story about an unknown incident and an unknown artist would be able to provoke people to think about the dangers of censorship.

Then, while visiting my friend Art Norris at his farm in Alberta, I was catching up on one of those books I'd always meant to read, *Reinventing Shakespeare*, a cultural history of The Bard. I was lounging in front of the fireplace when I discovered a passage about *Othello* and how, in 1692, Thomas Rymer deemed the play inappropriate to perform because it portrayed a black man in a position of military authority. I smiled at the irony. The irony, of course, was that in 1991—the year I was reading this passage—some academics were challenging *Othello*'s fitness for the stage because it portrayed a black man who was completely controlled by his jealousy and murdered his Caucasian wife in a fit of rage.

Perhaps, I thought, I should write a play about a black actor condemned for playing Othello.

Fortunately, I kept reading, started running into all the references to Shylock and decided I'd stick to my own cultural turf—for now—and write about Shakespeare's infamous Jew.

And although it shouldn't affect the way you read the play—yes, I am Jewish.

I hear the question, which is in the play and which I've certainly heard before. "With a name like Leiren-Young?"

Leiren is a name I took when I was a teenager after my stepfather, Hall Leiren, married my mother—then Carol Young. Young was originally Yankovich but my Zaida, Sid Young, changed it when he started high school in Regina, Saskatchewan. I asked him why and he recalls: "At that time it wasn't the "in thing" to have a name like Yankovich. Maybe today I wouldn't have changed it." His parents soon changed their names as well. It was easier to get by in those days with a name like Young.

I'm generally a fast writer but for some reason I could never quite convince myself to sit down and start this play. Fortunately, about six months after getting the initial idea, Vancouver's New Play Centre announced a 24-hour playwriting contest, so I entered. In a little less than a day I had my first draft.

It was fun to write but I knew that it wasn't much of a play. It was a rant without much plot or structure. I don't think my actor—the star of the show—even had a name.

It took me until 1994 to go back to the script in an attempt to provide story, structure and a name for the actor (then Joshua Richmond). Within the context of the play I found myself becoming less interested in censorship and more interested in exploring *The Merchant of Venice.* Unlike Jon Davies I'm not personally convinced Shakespeare is an anti-Semite simply because he created Shylock. After all, he also wrote *Hamlet* and I'm fairly certain he never killed a king. But anti-Semitisim was the fashion of his time, I certainly do not believe that the character of Shylock was created to promote goodwill towards Jews and I wanted to explore the possibility that perhaps Shakespeare's play *is* dangerous.

I still wasn't happy with what I'd written—I felt I'd now managed to create a play that had a story and structure but not much heart. I submitted it to Canada's National One Act Playwriting Competition hoping to get some feedback and instead of the constructive critique I'd been waiting for, received a cheque for second prize.

Over the next few years I kept working with the script, trying to make sure it wasn't just "about" censorship. The more time I spent with it, the more I realized that it was also about Shakespeare, Shylock, what it feels like for a Jew to be called a racist, and a man named Jon Davies.

But if you're reading, directing or acting this play feel free to decide what you think it's "about."

I hope you enjoy it. I hope it makes you think. And most of all, I hope it catches you up in the world of Jon Davies—and Shylock—until the book is closed or the curtain falls.

— Mark Leiren-Young, July 1996

John Huston as Jon Davies in the By the Book Western Canadian Tour of *Shylock*.

Shylock (1996)
and
The Merchant of Venice (1596)

After four centuries of performance, Shakespeare's *The Merchant of Venice* remains a barometer of social (in)sensitivity to racial hatred, an index of the theatre's response to the politically (in)correct, and a massive source of embarrassment and concern to the Jewish community. The questions it raises are voiced in the shrill but widely shared views of Professor Marcia T. Berman in Mark Leiren-Young's play: "The history of Shylock," she declares, "is the history of anti-Semitism. Why should anyone perform this play in this day and age? Why should anyone see this play?"

The "day and age" to which Marcia Berman refers are the here and now: post-Holocaust Canada in 1996, where there is no place for what she calls "this wretched piece of neo-Nazi propaganda"—especially when Nazism is resurgent in Germany and the Aryan Nations are spreading anti-Jewish hate messages via the Internet. In response, she calls for a form of social censorship: boycott the production in protest against the actor's vile portrayal of Shylock as a vicious Jewish villain.

The actor/protagonist, on the other hand, will have none of it. He protests eloquently against censorship in all its ugly forms, and resolutely refuses—in the name of truth and historical accuracy—to mitigate Shylock's cruelty by soft-soaping him as a wounded victim of Christian prejudice. With none of the carefully equivocating reservations of academic scholarship, Jon Davies deals head-on with the dreadful questions we hesitate to ask of the greatest of Renaissance humanists:

"Was Shakespeare an anti-Semite?

Of course he was.

That was the fashion of the day."

"The day," in this context, is a date in 1596—almost unimaginably remote from the world of modern political sensitivity towards women and Jews and racial minorities, but (like 1996) only four years away from that metaphoric shift into the future heralded by the *fin de siècle*. As early as the 1570s, those critics of an age about to leap from the late Middle Ages into the new world of Renaissance England were already lamenting the horrible changes lying in wait for humankind. The fears engendered in 1996 by (shall we say?) genetic engineering or technological invasions of our privacy, are replicated in the concerns expressed four centuries ago by a generation similarly terrified of the encroachment of modernity upon human nature.

The fears most manifestly apparent in *The Merchant of Venice* relate, of course, to the emergence of a moneyed class of upstart merchants with their brutal materialism, and the impact of the "new economics" upon the moral well-being of the community. The Church (for whom charity was the governing principle in money matters, and for whom the taking of interest was anathema) had been steadily losing power to the State (which could not function, in the modern world of trade and commerce, without borrowing money at interest). And the Usury Bill of 1571, establishing a 10% rate on loans, was a catastrophe to those who still held to the economic morality of the old medieval world. Shakespeare, I believe, was one of these. Another was an eloquent parliamentarian, Thomas Wilson, whose cry of anguish seems to resound as a subtext in *The Merchant of Venice*:

> [M]en have altogether forgotten free lending, and have geven themselves wholye to lyve by fowle gayning, making the lone of money a kinde of merchandise, a thinge directly against all lawe, against nature, and against God. And what should this meane, that, in steade of charitable dealing, and the use of alms . . . hardness of harte hath nowe gotten place, and greedie gayne is cheefelye followed, and horrible extortion commonly used? I do verely believe, the end of thuys worlde is nighe at hande.[1]

To be against law, nature and God was to be profoundly un-Christian and profoundly un-English. That is to say, it was to be quintessentially "other" or—as Shakespeare and his contemporaries understood the term— quintessentially "Jewish."[2]

History makes at least one fact clear: there was absolutely no "Jewish Problem" in England to which Shakespeare was responding in his putatively anti-Semitic play. England in 1596 was *Judenrein*, the Jews having been expelled by Edward I in 1290 and not readmitted until Cromwell—some 350 years later—snuck them in again by the back door. In their absence, however, the Jewish moneylenders who had been an invaluable source of revenue through taxation to the King, left behind them a stereotype built upon fear and loathing: the usurious "Jew" as Judas, the keeper of Christ's purse and treacherous unto death—regicide, deicide, and embezzler of his Master's treasury; the "Jew" as a living allegory of the Deadly Sins associated with moneylending—covetousness, greed, extortion, coin-clipping; the "Jew" as anti-Christ—avaricious to secure a debt by hacking off the flesh nearest to his sacrificial victim's heart.

Without necessarily setting eyes on a single Jew, Shakespeare was able to tap a deeply entrenched source of racial and religious hatred by bringing on this Devil in the likeness of a Jew. Why—when there was no Jewish Problem? If Shakespeare is to be accused of anything at all by the Marcia Bermans of the world, it is surely his *mauvais foi* that needs to be called to account: his deflection of a monumental "Christian Problem" upon an ancient stereotype of everything hatefully un-English. The real Devil of 1596 was the extortionate middle-class Christian moneylender whose rate of interest far exceeded the 10% maximum established by the Usury Bill of 1571.

One hears the outrage again and again in the writings and the plays of the period from the 1570s through the early seventeenth century: the accusation against the so-called *Kristen-Juden*—Christians who behave "Jewishly"—that they have become a curse even more heinous to society than the Jews:

> What is the matter that Jews were so universally hated whersoever they came? For soothe, usurie is one of the chief causes, for they rob all men that deal with them, and undo them in the end. And for this cause they were hated in England, and so banished worthily, with whom I would wish all these Englishmen were sent that lend their money or their goods whatsoever for gain, for I take them to be no better than Jews. Nay, shall I say: they are worse than Jews. (Thomas Wilson, *A Discourse Upon Usury*, 1572)

Jews seek to excel in Christianity and Christians in Jewishness.
(Robert Wilson, *The Three Ladies of London*, 1584)

'Tis less evil / In a state to cherish Jews, than Christian usurers.
(James Shirley, *The Gentleman of Venice*, 1632)

The Merchant of Venice, it seems to me, shares in this sense of profound misgiving about the rise of a mercantile middle-class that was displacing an impoverished aristocracy and substituting an ethic of unfeeling rapacity in the place of a "Christian" value system based upon generosity and charity. Shylock, together with the fairy tale suitors who come to court Portia in Belmont, incarnates a gross and ugly materialism that is so much a part of everyday business in 1996 that we no longer recognize it as such. Who's afraid of Shylock, now, for heaven's sake! He's our credit card, our bank manager, our mortgage company. And if he redefines a moral system in which "good" comes to mean "economically solvent," has this shocking and preposterous inversion not become habitual in our economic usage. One possible effect of *The Merchant of Venice* is that it may encourage us to recognize the universal Shylock beneath the skin.

We may continue, like Shakespeare, to dream of a Belmontian economy where we can afford to be sublimely contemptuous of filthy cash and disburse it in a spirit of lavish generosity with no concern for creditors. But Shylock's world is the hard reality of 1996: of profits derived from interest, of unsentimental trade and commerce, and a universal monetarism that takes little account of human consequence. Shylock is a terrible warning of the moral failure which permits profit and possession to supervene above brotherhood, human relationships, love, decency, mercy, and respect for human life. And Shylock belongs to a racist society which creates its own monsters—whatever name it chooses to give them. But only someone like Shylock himself, incapable of distinguishing between the world of metaphor and factual reality, could mistake him for a Jew without the quotation marks.

The Merchant of Venice, I have been suggesting, belongs to the history of a contemporary economic debate about the morality of money-lending which began centuries before the play was written and continued into the Commonwealth. One year after Shakespeare's play was performed, Francis

Bacon (as if in amused response to it) wrote his essay "Of Usurie" in which he took a sober and pragmatic attitude toward the controversy. His main contention was that it is pointless to demonize the taking of interest or ascribe the activity to "Judaizing." Economic necessity, trade, and a supply of capital must supervene over Antonio's outmoded notion that "it is against nature for money to beget money." He would seem to be siding with Shylock in the debate, even if one of the side-effects of these new economics is a hardness of heart that one might deplore. There is, for Bacon, no ubiquitous Superjew manipulating world finances. Times change, he implies, and we must leave behind the invectives and the foolish superstitions that cling to everything we hate and fear. But Shakespeare was incapable of relinquishing his "Jew." And *The Merchant of Venice* remains a deeply conservative cry of misgiving that the Renaissance will usher in a new century of strangers, alienated from their moral centre, indifferent to God as the Prime Economist, and unspeakably bourgeois in their dealings. Mark Leiren-Young's actor/protagonist, whatever the specifics of his argument for playing Shylock as a villain, is surely correct in his central line of reasoning. It makes no sense for *The Merchant of Venice* to dissociate its peculiar form of anti-Semitism—anachronistic, deeply superstitious, and in shockingly bad faith—from the economic causes that four hundred years ago made it credible.

One final point. "Jew"or Jew, Shylock is a bundle of human frailties that makes him far more than the sum of ancient Christian phobias. Jon Davies, in *Shylock*, has chosen to play him as a villain. But he has played him several times before—as an ethnic clown and as a victim of anti-Semitism crying out for acceptance—and, being a good actor, he has made these readings work in defiance of the play. Mark Leiren-Young's image of Shylock as a "layered" creation is vital. It suggests the archaeology of the role, the intertextual Shylocks who lurk beneath the surface and wait for the appropriate time and place to select their layered selves[3], the complexity of a character whose worst fault may have nothing at all to do with his "Jewishness." What I find most appalling about Shylock is his fatal equation of symbolic speech with literal factuality: his inability to distinguish between the "flesh and blood" (his daughter) that was stolen from him and the "flesh and blood" (a man's heart) that he demands as recompense for his loss. This madness has little to do with Old Testament legality, and even less with Talmudic commentary on eyes and teeth. He claims to have learned his principles of vengeance from the Christian community. But his brothers beneath the skin are neither Jews nor Christians. One of Shylock's many layers is the one he shares with those other doomed literalists in Shakespeare—Othello, Troilus, and even Antony and Cleopatra—who cross over the boundary that separates figurative speech from phenomenal reality and enact their madnesses as a form of tragic compulsion.

My response to Marcia Berman would be: "Never mind the 'Jew'. But beware the deranged literalist who pursues a crazy course of action on the basis of a grimly logical premise." That would also be my director's note to the actor. In 1997, however, I may change my mind.

Errol Durbach
Professor, Theatre Program
The University of British Columbia

---

1) Thomas Wilson, *A Discourse Upon Usury*, ed. R.H. Tawney (London: Geo. Bell and Sons Ltd., 1925), p. 177.

2) It is James Shapiro's thesis in *Shakespeare and the Jews* (New York: Columbia University Press, 1996), that "Englishness" in Shakespeare's world existed in sharp contradistinction to the idea of "Jewishness." Readers interested in pursuing the idea of "Jew" in *The Merchant of Venice* should consult this book.

3) For a good performance history of the Shylock role, see John Gross's book, *Shylock: A Legend and its Legacy* (New York: Simon & Schuster, 1992).

Preface

"The tyranny of open-mindedness often makes us silent."

When I first read *Shylock* in the Spring of 1994, I was immediately struck by the timeliness of the subject matter, the verbal density of the piece, and the challenges it posed as a piece of theatre. The conceit of the piece was simple and disarmingly straightforward: a well-known Shakespearean actor who has been playing Shylock in a production of *The Merchant of Venice* decides to participate in a talk-back session with the audience after a closing performance of what has been a bitterly controversial run of the play. The actor challenges the audience, the theatre establishment that has bowed to community pressure and cancelled the production, and most significantly, himself, about the pros and cons of presenting *The Merchant of Venice* in the socially sensitized environment that "enlightens" the latter years of the twentieth century.

In some ways that early draft read more like an imaginative lecture than a play, but the piece was clearly arresting enough to invite further involvement. How could one not be impressed by the timeliness of the subject matter? Like many of my colleagues in the arts, I was no stranger to the chilling effect that "political correctness" had been having on artistic endeavours for over a decade. (As if to underscore the ubiquitousness of this concern, not long after the completion of this play I read that no less prominent a theatrical luminary than the Artistic Director of the Stratford Shakespeare Festival was quoted as saying that he found it increasingly difficult in the present climate to even consider mounting plays like *The Merchant of Venice* and *The Taming of the Shrew*.)

I suppose we all have our horror stories about the excesses of social phenomena like political correctness and its cousins, cultural appropriation and racial stereotyping. I shudder to think what would have happened had George Ryga written *The Ecstasy of Rita Joe* in 1990. Would this play, which some consider a milestone in Canadian theatre, have made it to the stage at all? Would George Ryga have escaped calumny for daring, as a middle-aged male of Ukrainian roots, to write about the plight of a young native Canadian woman who is unable to cope with life in the big city? *Shylock* deals with many of these concerns head-on.

Initial response from the theatrical community confirmed what the playwright and I both felt, namely, that the play's subject matter was "on target," but that the character of the actor needed more development over the course of the play. Quite apart from humanizing the persona of the actor playing Shylock, there was also the matter of the play's structure and length. The playing time of that early draft was close to two hours, and, given that this one-person show would not be enhanced by its being presented with an interval, that was too long.

Over the past two years *Shylock* has undergone several transformations. For me, the biggest challenge was to be able to demonstrate, theatrically, some progression in the character of the actor playing Shylock. By the time we got to draft five that man had undergone a name change, an attitude adjustment, and his outward appearance evolved into a fully-costumed and made-up protagonist who, over the course of the play, sheds bits and pieces of his theatricality, until he stands before his audience, if not naked, then at least more vulnerable and human than he was when we first met him.

The play is about many things. Certainly it is about censorship vs. freedom of expression. It is also about a particular kind of censorship that I believe can be most insidious—self-censorship. For any artist in any discipline to feel he or she must inhibit the creative impulse to avoid social disgrace is deplorable. The thought that one might not produce a play, exhibit a canvas, broadcast a work or publish a novel on the grounds that it might be "perceived as offensive" is in danger of becoming a disturbing commonplace of our cultural universe. In this age of heightened awareness and virtually instant global communication, there is, to be sure, a greater degree of responsibility to be borne by artists when approaching "sensitive" material. But there is a dangerously thin line between respecting and accommodating the comfort threshold of "minority groups" and strangling the principle of freedom of speech. Finally, for me, *Shylock* is also about identity, and the lengths to which we, as individuals and as a society, will go to disguise that identity for as long as we can. It is about the "identity" of Jon Davies, who, in some respects, comes "out of the closet." It is as much about the epiphany of this actor, who happens to be Jewish, as it is about any individual who has the courage to raise issues so vital to all of us for whom freedom of expression is the cornerstone of our political and social existence.

—*John Juliani, Director*

The Cast:

JON DAVIES: An actor. Over 40. He is dressed as Shylock and when the play starts he is made up to the hilt, complete with ugly hook nose etc. which he removes over the course of the play. The play ends with him no longer in make-up. During the play Jon "quotes" or speaks for a few other characters but he doesn't need to mimic them. When he talks about Marcia T. Berman any affectation should be minimal, the actor shouldn't try to sound female or attempt a parody, the tone of voice can convey his attitude towards her ideas but let the character have her say; Tony Q. Fulford is British, so an accent would work well here.

THE TIME: Tomorrow.

SETTING: A stage. There are two options.

> #1. It is decked out for a full production
>   of *The Merchant of Venice*.
>
> #2. There is no set. The curtain is closed.

Shylock was first produced by Savage God at Vancouver's Bard On The Beach Shakespeare Festival on August 5, 1996. The role of Jon Davies was played by David Berner. The production was directed by John Juliani. Set design by Ronald Fedoruk; costume by Mara Gottler.

The American premiere of *Shylock* was February 24, 1998 at the Walnut Street Theatre in Philadelphia. The role of Jon Davies was played by William Leach who received a Barrymore nomination for his performance. It was directed by Deborah Block with set design by Thom Bumblauskas; costume design by Ashlynn Billingsley and lighting design by Troy A. Martin-O'Shia.

JON *enters. If you are using set #1 he enters from whichever building provides the grandest entrance. If you are using set #2 he enters from the side (so he doesn't have to part the curtains). As soon as he appears it should be apparent that he is in "full character" (and full make-up) as* SHYLOCK *and playing it for maximum villainous value. When he demands his "pound of flesh" the feel should be almost sexual—Caligula commanding the delivery of a virgin, the Devil anticipating the corruption of a pure soul. The desire should be electric.*

SHYLOCK: I wilt take his flesh to bait fish withal. If it will feed nothing else, it will feed my revenge. He hath disgrac'd me and hind'red me half a million; laughed at my losses, mock'd at my gains, scorned my nation, thwarted my bargains, cooled my friends, heated mine enemies. And what's his reason? I am a Jew. Hath not a Jew eyes? Hath not a Jew hands, organs, dimensions, senses, affections, passions; fed with the same food, hurt with the same weapons, subject to the same diseases, healed by the same means, warmed and cooled by the same winter and summer as a Christian is? If you prick us, do we not bleed? If you tickle us, do we not laugh? If you poison us, do we not die? And if you wrong us, shall we not revenge? If we are like you in the rest, we will resemble you in that. If a Jew wrong a Christian, what is his humility? Revenge. If a Christian wrong a Jew, what should his suffrance be by Christian example? Why, revenge. The villainy you teach me I will execute; and it shall go hard but I will better the instruction.

(SHYLOCK *savours his moment and then,*
taunting the audience . . .)

SHYLOCK: The pound of flesh which I demand of him is dearly bought, 'tis mine, and I will have it.

JON: Delicious. (pause) You can boo if you like. If it'll make you feel better. That is, after all, the "correct" response.

SHYLOCK: *(even nastier)* The pound of flesh which I demand of him is dearly bought, 'tis mine, and I will have it.

JON: For what it's worth that's also the response Shylock probably got back in Shakespeare's day—although back then people weren't booing him to show their outrage. Or their political sophistication. They were simply booing him because he was a villain. And a Jew. Not that there was a difference.

SHYLOCK: *(comically)* Oh my ducats. Oh my daughter. Oh my ducats.

JON: Is that better?

He takes off the first bit of Shylock make-up or costume.

JON: Hello, I'm Jon Davies.

Shylock.

And this . . . is our festival's regularly scheduled "talk-

back" session. I don't usually go to these things but tonight
. . . is different. Tonight I actually demanded the chance to
come out here after the show.

So why is this night different from all other nights?

Because tonight was our last performance of *The Merchant
of Venice.* That's right, the last performance, despite the
fact that if you check your programs—or my contract—
you'll see this show is scheduled to run for the next eight
weeks.

And that's what I want to talk about.

This is also going to be different for another reason. Usually
talk-backs are "question and answer" sessions, but after a
month in the public eye it seems to me that all the questions
have already been asked. So tonight I'm going to simply do
my best at coming up with the answers, to talk back. After
all, I've had a fairly difficult time doing that lately since it
seems like every time I open my mouth somebody starts to
boo or hiss or shout me down. So I thought this was the perfect opportunity—perhaps the only opportunity—to share
my perspective on our festival's little "controversy."

I had hoped that some of my fellow actors, or perhaps our
festival's wonderful director Tony Q. Fulford—you can
applaud if you like, I'm sure he'd be delighted—would be
joining us, but when they realized that some of our friends
from the media would be here with their television cameras and their microphones . . .

(He gestures in the direction of the "cameras" and bows.)

JON: And that they would undoubtedly be interviewing us afterwards . . . they all discovered they had other, more pressing, engagements.

That's why Tony was going to cancel tonight's talk-back session. Because no one else felt much like talking tonight. I suppose no one else wanted to stand up here and risk making any public statements that could get them branded as "racists." Like me.

But Tony said that if I really wanted to do this . . . "Well, just try and behave yourself."

So if you were looking forward to meeting Tony or asking our Portia, Bev Argosy, about her role in the soap opera *All My Children*, then feel free to leave now. Don't worry, I won't be offended.

(beat) Thank you.

And if you were hoping for a chance to quiz me—or abuse me—I'd appreciate it if you'd wait until after I've said my piece.

If you've read the program notes you'll know that I have played Shylock before. Three times now actually. In fact I played the part at this very festival seven years ago. So I generally have no problem discussing the character, the play or the production which, for the record, I am very proud of.

Although I must confess that after persuading Tony to let me do this session tonight I almost came up with a pressing post-show engagement myself. The last time I tried to talk about this I didn't do so well. But then I thought about it for a bit and decided it wouldn't be fair if someone didn't make sure that all the lovely reporters—and anyone out there who is upset about our production—got their pound of flesh. That is, after all, the sticking point isn't it? That damned pound of flesh. Ah, there's the rub. The Jew as moneylender. The Jew as Christ killer. The damned Jew . . . If not for that one pound of flesh *Merchant* would just be one big happy family comedy.

SHYLOCK: *(savage)* The pound of flesh which I demand of him is dearly bought, 'tis mine, and I will have it.

JON: When it comes down to it that pound of flesh is why we—why the festival—added these nightly talk-back sessions. You see, as many of you know, we added these nightly apologies two weeks ago, after our production had officially become "controversial." After the nasty letters to the papers started.

The original plan was to do these sessions once a week and I actually had it written into my contract that I didn't have to attend any of them. I don't mind doing them after the school matinees, although the questions at those tend to be fairly predictable—"How do you learn all those lines?" and "Who built the set?" And, I must admit, there are always a few interesting ones after this play.

But I like to think an adult audience is capable of thinking through issues without the help of a "guided discussion" or a "facilitator." The way I see it, if you have something to say, do your own play and say it. Although for those of you wondering, the set was built by professional stage carpenters. And as for how we learn all those lines—practice.

But I suppose that's how we produce "controversial" plays these days, isn't it? We create a safety net so no one gets upset and writes a nasty letter to the board of directors. Or a lot of nasty letters. And a petition.

That's why, at the beginning of the show, Tony came out to make a little apology to you all. That was always part of the production by the way. He doesn't call it an apology of course. He tells you it's an introduction, his special oh-so-charming *(as Tony)* "Welcome to the theatre." And in this welcome he reminds you what a difficult piece of work this really is and what it's all about and how you're supposed to feel when it's over.

Apparently they have to do that these days because they're afraid the audience will be so surprised by seeing something meaningful or relevant in a theatre that you may find yourself completely disoriented by the experience. And, of course, by giving you fair warning and letting you know what to expect it's all so much safer, isn't it? Like the flight attendant telling you about all the emergency exits and the oxygen masks just before takeoff. And now we even get to talk to you again after the play—just to make sure you don't go out with any . . . incorrect impressions. The whole premise seems to be that we don't trust audiences to think about things on their own. Or maybe we just don't trust you to think at all. Personally, I always thought it was a play's job to provoke you and your job to figure out what it all means. Be careful what you wish for.

Years ago I was one of the founders of a group called Theatre of Blood. Somebody here must remember it . . . Then again.

There were about a dozen of us, just out of university, and we were into "confrontational" theatre. One piece . . . we put the audience into an old warehouse with no seats, locked all the doors, shoved them around and pointed guns at them for two hours to simulate the experience of being held hostage by terrorists. After the show, after all our shows, we'd sit around in a circle and "process" the experience. But then I grew up and decided it was possible to create effective theatre without actually causing the audience physical harm, and there was no reason that once the show was over they couldn't go out for a coffee and "process it" for themselves. But obviously in this age of childproof caps and warning labels on fresh fruit it was only a matter of time before we had to start standing up here after every play to make sure you understood what you just saw.

So, just to make sure that no one goes home and tries to abuse a Jewish money-lender, the actors come out after the show to help you "process" the experience. At least that's the theory. That's what I thought was going on.

Then, one night, I sat in—sat backstage actually—to hear what sort of questions were asked. To see how my colleagues were defending the play. Defending me.

And, to be honest, that was another big reason I didn't want to go along with these "talk-backs" once the controversy started. I'm the one all the fuss is about and I didn't feel right about defending my own work.

Maybe I should have. Maybe then they wouldn't have cancelled the show.

But what can I say? I'm a genius? That I'm doing a wonderful job with the part? My performance is inspired? That what I'm doing on stage is "art?"

I'm an actor. That means I think I'm brilliant while I'm onstage and in the bar afterwards and incompetent when I'm driving home, picturing all the things I could have done better.

Seriously, how the hell should I know if what I'm doing is art? How do any of us know? But I know that what Shakespeare did is art. That I'm comfortable with.

So I sat backstage and listened and I couldn't believe the questions. Almost none of them about the play or the production—most of them about the actors. And then, just when they were trying to wrap things up, an old woman stands up and asks why the festival had chosen to do *Merchant* in the first place. "Why not something nice like

Comedy of Errors or *Hamlet*?" She was upset. "Isn't this play anti-Semitic? Isn't the portrayal of Jews like this dangerous?"

And then Bev says she doesn't see what the problem is. "After all, there are plenty of nasty characters in Shakespeare. There are plenty of nasty characters in *Measure for Measure*. So what makes this so different?"

What's so different? Well, first off—no character in *Measure for Measure* is identified as "the Jew." And suddenly I'm thinking that if this is the best we can do at defending *Merchant* then maybe people are right, maybe we shouldn't be doing it.

But then I hear that distinctive *harumph* and I know the boss is jumping in to save the day. I can feel my blood pressure lowering as soon as I realize he's about to speak. Tony Q. to the rescue. And what's the official defense? Why are we doing *Merchant of Venice*? "Because it's Shakespeare."

That was it. Because it's part of the mythic canon.

And I realized that's always been my explanation.

And maybe that's enough. Maybe before all *this* that would have been enough. But after all the . . . controversy . . . I was hoping for something with a little more substance.

And then someone asks about me—about my Shylock—and

whether it isn't "too negative." And Tony . . . my director, my friend, says maybe my portrayal is "a touch on the negative side, but Shylock is a very complicated character." Tony, the same director who put this show together and sat down with me and agreed on this "negative approach." And that was all he said.

Then another question—is the show anti-Semitic? *(as Tony)* "I don't think so." And a few people laughed and then he started plugging the festival's production of *Much Ado*.

That was our official defense.

So I asked Danny, our stage manager, what these things were usually like. He says this one was "pretty intense."

This one was intense?

Danny tells me the cast usually fields about a dozen questions—and you know what they talk about most? You know what everyone's biggest concern is? The time Bev Argosy got to do a nude scene with Johnny Depp.

I know—exciting isn't it.

But I'm not sure it gets quite to the heart of what this play is about. I'm not sure that exactly "deals with the issues."

The issues.

It's opening night, just over a month ago and we're all in

the lounge for the *(as Tony)* "post-show gala." And I'm talking to a friend when I see this woman looking at me. She's mid-thirties, well dressed, with shoes that cost more than my car. So I figure her for a board member.

I smile. She does not smile back. But she comes over to the table and she has this look on her face like she wants something. I think maybe she wants an autograph. *(defensively)* It happens.

So I turn to her and smile again, but before I can introduce myself she launches into this tirade about *Merchant*, what a terrible play this is and what a horrible thing I'm doing on stage. How what I'm doing is dangerous. How I'm clearly a bigot. And . . . an anti-Semite.

An anti-Semite?

I start to laugh. And she wants to know what's so funny.

And I tell her I'm Jewish.

I'm expecting her to be embarrassed. But instead she looks at me—the way the Venetians look at Shylock in the play. No. Angrier than that. And she asks how I can be Jewish with a name like Davies. Talk about stereotyping. So I tell her that when my grandmother arrived in North America, the bureaucrat who filled out her paperwork thought it was easier to spell than Davidovich. As for Jon I shortened that name myself. I never liked Jonathan.

Then she tells me I'm a "traitor" to my race—a traitor—and a self-hating Jew.

Excuse me?

"How could you?" she says.

How could I what?

"How could you?" And then she spit at me. She missed, but she spit at me.

I couldn't believe it. How do you respond to that? What do you say?

Then she says I'll be hearing from her. And that I'll be hearing from her friends. And as she storms out the door I realize the whole room is looking at me, waiting for me to do something, so I just say "everybody's a critic." And everyone laughs and starts talking again and it's all better. But I know it's not.

The first time I did an old style melodrama I played a villain and I was so thrilled when the audience booed and hissed just like they were supposed to. It was such a treat to get a real reaction. And when I played the villain in Aladdin, I was delighted when the children screamed. That's what it's all about, isn't it? Make people laugh, make them cry, get them angry, make them think.

But make them spit at you? After the show is over? After

you've taken off the make-up and gone to the bar to relax? Bad reviews are one thing, but this?

Then, two days later, it happened.

(He takes out a neatly trimmed page of newspaper.)

I'm sure you've all read it by now. I'm beginning to suspect that everyone in the world has read it by now. I had phone calls from people I hadn't heard from in decades asking if I'd seen it, just so they could hear my reaction. But in case you missed it—for some reason this letter wasn't posted on our review board—here it is . . . "Merchant an Insult to All."

You've got to love those headlines. Not just an insult to my new friend, not even just an insult to Jews. An insult to all.

"Yesterday, I found myself assaulted by a production of Shakespeare's *Merchant of Venice*."

Assaulted. Someone being attacked by a gang outside a 7-11, that's assault. A play—even a bad play—assault?

Then she goes on about being a long-time season ticket holder and after that she really starts in. "I've always questioned the validity of this festival's," quote, 'obligation,' unquote—quotation marks hers—"to produce all of Shakespeare's works, including material that is clearly substandard, unfinished or simply hackneyed—and works which have little or no relevance to a modern audience. I can appreciate that some may feel it is important to produce these 'classics.'" The word classics is, of course, also in quotation marks—"despite the fact that many of the opinions and attitudes expressed are clearly offensive by modern standards, e.g. last season's screamingly misogynistic production of *Taming of the Shrew*."

For the record, I was in that and it was a fine production—despite what the critics said.

"But while I can appreciate that some may feel it is important to expose us to the entire Shakespearean repertoire I still found myself stunned—and appalled—by the current production, which is clearly an example of hate literature masquerading as theatre.

"I can find no reason why someone would produce this play, a play that holds Jews up to scorn and ridicule, in the current climate of hostility towards Jews and the State of Israel.

"It is bad enough that Shylock—who is constantly referred to as "the Jew"—is a stereotypical moneylender and that the only salvation available to his daughter, Jessica, is conversion to Christianity, but the playing of Shylock in this production is unforgivable.

"Jon Davies is a Sturmer cartoon come to life. His vile portrayal of a Jew who licks his lips hungrily at each reference to money, his refusal to imbue the character with even an ounce of humanity in his search for a pound of flesh"—there's that damn pound of flesh again—"is clearly the work of someone who not only wishes to forget his own heritage but to deny it entirely.

"The history of *Merchant* is the history of anti-Semitism. Why should anyone perform this play in this day and age? Why should anyone see this play? What makes this play any different, any more important, any more essential to our spiritual well-being than any of the other thousands of formula romantic comedies about lovers that Shakespeare and his Elizabethan cronies churned out?

"This production is not theatre, it a cruel attack against the Jewish people of this community and an insult to anyone who prides themselves on being fair-minded and tolerant. Anyone who truly believes in racial equality must refuse to attend and thereby support this wretched piece of neo-Nazi propaganda and should boycott this festival until such time as the final curtain falls on this truly hateful production.

"Signed, Professor Marcia T. Berman."

Vile portrayal. Neo-Nazi propaganda. Hate literature masquerading as theatre. Deny my own heritage . . . I preferred it when she spit at me.

A pause as he removes another layer of make-up.

I suspect it was the word "boycott" that made someone on the board suggest the "talk-back sessions" should become a nightly event.

15

I don't usually pay much attention to reviews. I won't lie and say I don't read them. Everybody reads them—and I think the people who swear they don't read them usually have them memorized—but in this case I expected the festival would respond. I waited for the festival to respond. It's one thing to say the show is bad or that I did a bad job, but to accuse me of being a Nazi propagandist, to accuse Shakespeare of being a Nazi propagandist . . . I was certain someone would defend the show, defend Shakespeare, defend me.

Bev told me I should take it as a compliment. *(as Bev)* "You should be pleased with yourself. You obviously struck a nerve." Actually, most of the cast was quite excited about it. Controversy. That's the way to sell tickets. Controversy. If you want to have TV stations talk about your production, see if you can get it picketed. Never fails.

Fine. It'll sell tickets. But what about these charges? What about being called a Nazi? Wasn't anyone else upset?

No. No one else was upset.

Maria Cornelli, the lovely eighteen-year-old Catholic girl playing my sweet Jewish daughter says to me, "Nazi, that's like a racist isn't it?"

"Yes," I said, "that's like a racist. Only more so." I suspect the only Nazis Maria had ever seen were in reruns of *Hogan's Heroes*.

No, no one else was upset. I suppose no one else ever spent a sleepless night wondering about their friends in Israel the last time a bomb exploded on a bus in Tel Aviv.

Maybe Marcia T. Berman did.

So I tried to be sensitive. I tried to think of the first time I saw *Merchant*. It was summer, just after my second year of theatre school. I was visiting England and I made the pilgrimage to Stratford. I should probably remember the name of the actor, but I've never been good with names. I suppose he looked Jewish, but like a Jewish clown, a borscht belt comedian, a Jackie Mason Jew. And that's how he played the role. I didn't think he was that funny but he got a lot of laughs, so whatever he was doing must have been working. I wasn't insulted. It didn't seem any different to me than watching Jewish comedians making jokes about their wives, mothers, chicken soup, Goyim and feeling persecuted and neurotic. It was no more offensive to me as a Jew than watching Woody Allen.

So the first time I played Shylock I played him as a clown, a fool, an ethnic fool. That's what I wanted, it's what the director wanted. It worked, but the play didn't. It's wrong. Comic relief. A few years later I had another shot at the role. At this very festival. The director decided Shylock was motivated by hurt, by his pain at being abused by the Christians. This was a sympathetic Shylock—a wounded Jew, a victim of anti-Semitism who was crying out for acceptance.

David Berner in the Vancouver premiere, Bard On The Beach, 1996.

SHYLOCK: *(oozing sympathy)* Signor Antonio, many a time and oft in the Rialto you have rated me about my moneys and my usances; still have I borne it with a patient shrug, for suff'rance is the badge of all our tribe; you call me misbeliever, cut-throat dog and spit upon my Jewish gaberdine, and all for use of that which is mine own. Well then, it now appears you need my help; go to, then; you come to me, and you say "Shylock, we would have moneys."

JON: This was a Shylock even Marcia T. Berman could love. A pathetic victim, a man deserving of our sympathies. Because that's my first impulse isn't it? That's every actor's first impulse, right—to make their character sympathetic. Everyone's the hero of their own story. Claudius believes he deserves the throne. Goneril knows she's only doing what's best for the kingdom. So, of course, Shylock knows he's a man who has been gravely wronged. And when someone attacks, the first impulse is to defend, to cry "*No!*" Shylock is not an evil man, *Merchant* is not a nasty play, it's ultimately a demand that the audience accept Shylock's humanity, that the audience accept that while he may be a Jew, that whichever God he may worship, that . . .

SHYLOCK: (*As sensitive as possible.*) If you prick us, do we not bleed? If you tickle us, do we not laugh?

JON: So that's what you say, what you're supposed to say, and what Marcia T. Berman and many of you here tonight would probably like me to say in order to "justify" a modern production of the play. That's the safe "correct" response, isn't it? Claim sympathy for the victim, for Shylock, and make you all feel like fools for missing the real point of the play regardless of how we play it. That's what the Talk-back session was really all about. That's why I was so offended by it. The whole idea was to reassure you, like Shakespeare does at the end of *Midsummer Night's Dream*, that "if we shadows have offended, think but this and all is mended, that you have but slumbered here while these visions did appear."

If I tell you that's what it's about, that it's really a play about understanding and respect then it's still valid today, isn't it—and it's your fault for misunderstanding it all. Then it's still important. It's the perfect defense. So that's it. *Merchant of Venice* is actually a statement about equality but Shakespeare knew his audience wasn't prepared to accept the idea of equality. So he played to his audience's prejudices even though he was still trying to challenge them. And when the Venetians abuse Shylock we're meant to see how ugly and hypocritical they are and how any evil within Shylock is all because of the way he's been treated by the insensitive Christians. It's a wonderful argument . . . absolute bullshit, but a wonderful argument.

Was Shakespeare an anti-Semite?

Of course he was.

That was the fashion of the day.

SHYLOCK: I hate him for he is a Christian, but more for that in low simplicity he lends out money gratis and brings down the rate of usance here with us in Venice. If I can catch him once upon the hip, I will feed fat the ancient grudge I bear him.

JON: That's a sympathetic character? That's the best Shakespeare can do at creating a sympathetic character?

If Iago was a member of a minority group would scholars be searching for subtext trying to prove Shakespeare simply thought he was misunderstood? I know—

SHYLOCK: (*as beautifully as possible*) Hath not a Jew eyes? Hath not a Jew hands, organs, dimensions, senses, affections, passions; is he not fed with the same food, hurt with the same weapons, subject to the same diseases, healed by the same means, warmed and cooled by the same winter and summer, as a Christian is? If you prick us, do we not bleed? If you tickle us, do we not laugh? If you poison us, do we not die?

JON: But as Signor Antonio says, "Even the devil can cite scripture for his purposes."

And what affectionate nickname does everyone use for Shylock?

The devil.

And what comes next—after this beautiful plea for love and tolerance?

SHYLOCK: And if you wrong us, shall we not revenge?

JON: Oh that's sweet isn't it? Very sympathetic.

It would be lovely to pretend Shakespeare wasn't a bigot; that he was trying to point out Shylock's wounded inner child; that Shylock is some sort of anti-hero; that if I'd been alive in his day, Bill and I could have hung out together at the tavern. Or that if he were alive today I could take him to a kosher style deli for some pastrami on rye or a couple of cheese blintzes. But somehow I doubt it.

Maybe he did have some kind thoughts about Jews, although since all the Jews had been exiled from England because they—we—were considered a threat to national security, chances are he'd never met one. And maybe he was trying to make his audience think about prejudice—just a bit. Hey, I'd like to think so too. But can you really look at this play and believe Shakespeare was writing this as a plea for tolerance?

In the trial scene the lovers refer to Shylock as Jew, not as Shylock. The same way they use the word "bastard" for Edmund in *Lear*, as if that one word can define his entire character—which for that audience, in that era, it did. Shylock isn't an individual any more, just a type—an evil type. The villain. Shakespeare offered more dimension, more humanity—even real motivation—but Shylock was a villain all the same who could only be cured, who could only be allowed to live, if he agreed to convert to Christianity. And as far as Shakespeare and his audience were concerned he was every bit as out of place and ugly in the beautiful lover's world of Venice as Bottom is in the faerie kingdom of Titania.

Besides, why is it the only "acceptable" portrayal of Shylock is as victim? Isn't that more offensive? If the idea is to break away from stereotypes I'd prefer fear to pity. To ignore the truth of the character—to play Shylock like a buffoon—that's offensive. If he's going to be a villain, let him be a villain.

I've studied my history. I know the reason so many Jews used to loan money was because it was one of the few jobs they were allowed to do. Because they—we—were considered infidels, we were consigned to the jobs our Christian brethren considered unworthy or dirty—like moneylender, undertaker or butcher. And the reason Jews had money to loan was that often we weren't allowed to buy property. And not just in Shakespeare's time.

My father came from a town near Odessa and the only reason he was permitted to own land was because his father, my grandfather, was a soldier for twenty-five years and was therefore considered a "citizen." And the only reason my grandfather was allowed to join the army and remain in it for twenty-five years was because until it was time for retirement, no one had realized that he was a Jew. No one had asked and he'd never volunteered the information.

So maybe Shylock wasn't allowed to own property, with the possible exception of his own home in the ghetto. He certainly wasn't allowed to enter most professions. He probably wasn't even allowed on the Rialto. He was taunted, robbed, attacked, spit on and "spurn'd like a strange cur." All because he was a Jew. And I'm sure if my good friend Marcia T. Berman had known I knew all that, I'm sure she would have been even more emphatic when she asked, "How could you?"

And the answer is that maybe if I thought of him as a Jew first I couldn't. I know Jew is a layer, an essential layer, perhaps the essential layer, but instead of making it the base of the character, I wanted to find the character Shakespeare had created. Not the character I would create as a twenty-first century Jew, or as a twenty-first century actor, or a twenty-first century liberal—but the character as it was actually written.

My first real acting instructor, Gary Loffleur, had the academic's view of Shakespeare. He didn't believe the genius was in the stories or the dramatic action, or even in the characters—it was all in the words, the poetry, the music. "When you speak those words they should slide along your tongue like the bubbles from a sip of champagne. And each syllable has it's own spice." That was Gary. Soliloquies were supposed to taste like fine chocolates, an entire play was a banquet.

I fell in love with Shakespeare for the stories. Not the words.

When I visited my grandmother at the home, when I was a kid, I always used to stare at her bookshelf—which was mostly cluttered up with pictures of family, photo albums and just three books: the Torah—that's the old testament— a prayer book and Shakespeare. It had well-worn red leather bindings and the spine had an etching of a man's face, Shakespeare's face, although I didn't know that at the time. I thought it was a picture of a sorcerer, perhaps even Merlin. And I thought the book was a collection of magic spells. My grandmother was so old that for all I knew she used to be friends with Merlin.

So on my thirteenth birthday my Grandmother gave me her copy of *The Collected Works* and I was delighted. Until I went into my bedroom with my new treasure, opened it up and discovered it was just a bunch of stupid, boring plays written in very strange English. There weren't even any pictures. I was heartbroken.

The closest I got to "literature" was *Batman*.

So I put the book on my shelf and I probably would have forgotten all about it if not for a severe case of the measles about a year later. It took me two days to reread all my comic books.

On day three I started *King Lear*.

I didn't understand all the words, I didn't understand most of the words, but somehow I managed to understand the story because at about midnight—as Lear cradled his poor, lifeless Cordelia in his arms—I began to cry. And it was the first time a story in a book ever made me cry. It wasn't Merlin—but it was magic all the same.

But even though I fell in love with Shakespeare for the stories, the words came a close second. They may not taste like champagne or chocolate—not to me anyway—but there's something very . . . fulfilling . . . about speaking them. They make me feel like the dream-speaker of the tribe, like I'm saying something that may be, or ought to be, or simply was and shouldn't be forgotten.

Fulfilling. Certainly more fulfilling than that allergy commercial I did a few months ago. You know the one.

(He does an over-sized sneeze.)

Except the allergy commercial paid more than a full season at the festival.

So when the Festival approached me about playing Shylock, Tony and I talked about the play and agreed—this would be an attempt to do Shylock the way he was written. So instead of starting with Jew—I started with villain. Instead of starting with outcast, I started with greed. And vengeance. And the type of villain Shakespeare's audience would have hated and booed and hissed. Much the same way some people in the audience for this show have hated and booed and hissed. The type of villain Shakespeare actually wrote. Yes, a negative character.

I've looked at the great Shylocks in history. At Macklin and Kean and the others who had played him through the ages. And all the greats had started with the same impulse—either a clown, who the world would laugh at, or a tragic and sympathetic old man. A man worn down by the wrongs of society. A man the audience could pity and perhaps even love because, melodramas aside, all actors want to be loved.

But almost all these men ultimately changed their approach. The longer they played the role the more apparent it became that Shylock isn't a wronged hero or a pathetic old man—he's the villain. And maybe there are moments the audience is meant to feel for him, but no more than they're meant to briefly feel for Richard the Third.

If Shakespeare truly meant to create a story about a sympathetic Jew, if he truly wanted to create a plea for tolerance, surely he wouldn't have told the story of a cruel Jewish moneylender who lives for vengeance. Moneylender—a profession lower on the social ladder in his day than prostitute. Or actor. If Shakespeare wanted us to accept the Jew as human, why praise Jessica for her "Christian temperament?" Why abuse and humiliate Shylock and demand that he convert?

Art is about truth. If theatre is still supposed to be art and not simply entertainment, then it's about truth. And as much as I may want to deny Shakespeare's attitude towards Jews, as much as Marcia T. Berman may want to deny the historical existence of Elizabethan anti-Semitism, as much as I may want this to be about forcing the Christians in this play, and the Christians watching this play, to confront the way Jews have been mistreated, this wasn't written about a Jew who was wronged by society. It's about a Jewish villain. A Jewish fiend. A Jewish devil.

No, the other characters aren't exactly world-class role models either but they are the heroes of the play and Shakespeare's audience was rooting for them to live happily ever after.

Before I started, as part of my character work—and I'm proud to say that yes, I still do character work—I picked up a copy of *The Jew of Malta*. And Marlowe's Jew makes Shylock look like Seinfeld. No ambiguity here, no hints of persecution. The name, "Jew" is clearly synonymous with evil. He may just as well have used the word "vampire." Shakespeare's Jew may wish his daughter dead but Marlowe's Jew, Barabas, poisons his daughter, poisons an entire nunnery.

This was Marlowe's big hit—a genuine crowd pleaser—and it's a horrifying play, every bit as horrifying as *Tamburlaine* or the existing fragments of *Edward the Second*, and every bit as brilliant. But since the play is by Marlowe, not Shakespeare, and the evil Jew is the title character, I wouldn't be surprised if one day the latest edition of the collected works of Marlowe is missing this particular script. Or if it's locked in special collections and only made available to selected scholars. One day it'll just disappear from the permanent record to make sure nobody is ever offended again.

It's not that much of a leap. First they came for *Merchant*, but I find anti-Semitism offensive so I said nothing. Then they came for *Taming of the Shrew*, but I find sexism offensive so I said nothing. Then they came for *Macbeth* for defaming the Scots and *Hamlet* for being unfair to the mentally ill. But maybe that isn't going far enough. If Elizabethan attitudes are offensive to modern sensibilities, perhaps we should just wipe out the entire Elizabethan era. Don't just do away with Shakespeare, make like Stalin and tear all the offending pages out of all our books . . . drama, literature, history.

Perhaps we could find a new guardian of taste to replace the great Bowdler, the patron saint of self-righteous censorship.

Bowdler. Clearly a woman before her time.

(He starts to remove another layer of make-up.)

I learned about Bowdler back with Theatre of Blood. We did a play about her ghost coming back to try and justify what she'd done.

Henrietta Bowdler, for those of you who never saw our production—and if I remember correctly only a few dozen people did—was a woman living just before the Victorian era who discovered that there were *(mock horror)* "dirty words" and "sexual references" scattered throughout the works of the Bard himself. In a fit of unbridled decency, Henrietta decided to produce a new version of Shakespeare's texts—one that would be fit for children and ladies. The only problem was it would have been improper for a lady as upstanding as herself to admit to having read and understood all the hetero- and homosexual references, that she had been so carefully removing from the texts of the Great Pornographer of the Elizabethan era. So, in order to protect her reputation, Henrietta asked her brother Tom to sign his name to the new G-rated editions of *Hamlet* and *Romeo and Juliet*. But it was the delicate Henrietta who decided which words, phrases and allusions were too risqué for impressionable minds and, in doing so, she created one of the best-selling books of the Victorian era.

Other people "fixed" Shakespeare too, which is a good term for it. "Fixed," as in neutered. A man named Tate believed his audience couldn't handle tragedy, because tragedy is just too sad, so Tate rewrote all the endings. So in Tate's *Lear*, Cordelia lives.

As a thirteen-year-old boy I think I would have preferred Tate's ending, although I doubt I would have been intrigued enough after seeing the Lear family live happily ever after to have bothered to read the rest of the book. Mind you, if Cordelia had lived, *Lear* would have a much better chance of being turned into a major motion picture. And if Horatio could provide Hamlet with an antidote for the poison, it would be so much easier to produce *Hamlet II—Return of the Great Dane*.

Tate would have been perfect for Hollywood. As Gary Loffleur used to say, every generation gets the Shakespeare they deserve. And perhaps we deserve Marcia T. Berman's Shakespeare, a Shakespeare where Shylock is the type of role model Jewish parents would like to see running their children's summer camps.

And why stop at Shakespeare? What about *Commedia* and its Pantalone, Moliere and his *Miser*. Chaucer and his *Canterbury Tales*. Orwell was an anti-Semite, so *1984* will have to go. Along with anything by Mencken and Fitzgerald. H.G. Wells hated Jews. So did T.S. Eliot, Victor Hugo and half the icons of English literature. So we can forget about *The Time Machine*, *The Invisible Man*, *The Great Gatsby* and maybe, if we're lucky, *Cats* and *Les Miserables*.

Mark Twain, one of the most liberal writers of his era, is now a bigot because he used "the N-word" in *Huckleberry*

Finn—a book about tolerance but why should that matter. Lewis Carroll was inordinately fond of little girls and Poe married his younger cousin just like Jerry Lee Lewis, so their work should be banished from the libraries. Conan Doyle liked cocaine, Coleridge was an opium addict, Hemingway a suicide—bad role models each and every one. You think I'm kidding. The next thing you know people will be protesting *Showboat.*

If you can't separate the artist and the art then if the artist is inappropriate surely we have to destroy their art.

And then I suppose it's time to ban the story of that greedy moneygrubber who abuses his employees, hates his family, terrifies small children and mocks Christian beliefs and the very concept of Christian charity. Yes, my friends, it is time to do away with Ebenezer Scrooge. Oh, I know Scrooge is never actually referred to as a Jew but is it that difficult to believe that Dickens, the same man who wrote the vicious character of Fagin—who is referred to as "The Jew" if you bother to read the book instead of just watching reruns of *Oliver* on TV—wasn't trying to create his own version of Shylock when he created Scrooge, the happy tale of an evil pointy-nosed devil who is redeemed and converted, although not necessarily in that order, after discovering the true spirit of the birthday of Christ. I know, I know, it also deals with hope and redemption and the healing power of love, but if Scrooge is a Jew—and I defy you to look at Alastair Sim and tell me he couldn't be playing a Victorian era Shylock—then why should this work be allowed to escape the sensitivity police?

Ebenezer—an ancient Hebrew name by the way, is haunted by the death of his partner Jacob—Yakov—the name of one of the three forefathers of the Jewish religion.

Ban *A Christmas Carol* now! Alastair Sim must be stopped.

As I'm sure most of you know, two weeks ago a group—it seemed like a hundred people, but it was probably no more than thirty, that's what the paper guessed anyway— stood outside with their picket signs. And then, when the show started, they came inside and booed each time I came on stage. Sorry, each time Shylock came on stage. I know, I shouldn't take these things so personally. And with each boo I thought I could see the spirit of Henrietta Bowdler lurking in the wings like the ghost of Denmark's dead king. And like Hamlet I was desperate to know what she wanted from me.

The next time I play Richard I fully expect a hunchback rights organization to demand that the King straighten up— or at least be shown to have some redeeming social qualities. You think I'm kidding. A school teacher in England refused to let her class attend the ballet *Romeo and Juliet* because of, quote, blatant heterosexual content. A school board, in America—in New Hampshire—stopped teaching *Twelfth Night* because it promotes cross-dressing.

And you know, when I heard them boo I wanted to stop the play and shout at them—to defend Shakespeare, to defend the play, our production. To do something.

After my first scene Danny comes up to me backstage, asks (*as Danny*) "What's going on? What should we do?" And I figure there's really only one thing to do, isn't there? So when I go back on stage in Act Two, before I speak my first line, I turn towards the audience, face them and smile, showing as much contempt for them as I can muster.

And after they've booed and hissed and some of the fine upstanding citizens have cried "shame" I nodded to acknowledge them, bowed deeply in gratitude (*he does so*), saluted (*he does so, then rises*) and returned to my role.

In a world where talk show guests can claim the Holocaust never happened, Klansmen can run for President of the United States and the leader of the United Nations turns out to be a former Nazi, there are two dozen people spending their evening in the theatre protesting a production of *Merchant of Venice*. I suppose I should be flattered.

But when I saw the story in the paper the next day talking about the audience reaction and the recent subscription cancellations by forty-five season ticket holders—and the accompanying editorial suggesting that perhaps Marcia T. Berman is right, perhaps the festival should remove *Merchant* from its repertoire—when I saw that I knew it couldn't be solved with a simple sarcastic bow.

The same editors who will fight to the death for a free press, the public's right to know and the freedom to publish the most obscenely intimate details of a sexual abuse trial were suggesting that perhaps it wasn't proper to expose our children—or even our adults—to dangerous authors like Shakespeare in this hypersensitive day and age. And this time I knew someone had to respond. I knew someone from the festival would come to our defense. That we would hold a press conference, issue a statement, say something.

And again, no one did.

And that was even worse to me than the letter. After all, am I supposed to be mad at the generals who lead the battle, the politicians who set the agenda, or the Good Germans who blindly follow orders?

But I kept hoping. And when I picked up the newspaper each morning last week I turned first to the letters to the editor, then to the theatre section, then to the columnists who usually jump at every opportunity to defend even the most inane of liberal causes. And the columnists were still writing their columns about gallery openings, controversial motion pictures and free speech for journalists in Central America, but not a word about the local production of *Merchant of Venice*. But then I realized . . . no one else wanted to risk being labeled a racist.

So last Friday I got my wish and Marcia T. Berman got hers. The theatre finally issued a statement. A termination notice. We would all be fully paid but the show would close. Tonight.

I went in to see our fearless leader. The venerable Tony Q.

Fulford. I didn't have to say anything, just stare at him.

(*as Tony*) "We have to answer to our board of governors. And many members of our board are . . . your people."

My people?

"You know."

Jews?

He nodded.

My people. And have they asked you to cancel it?

He shook his head.

But you don't believe they'll be disappointed with your decision? He shifted his eyes away, staring at the ground like a servant in a badly directed Restoration comedy.

Don't you see what you're doing here? Don't you see what you're starting?

"I'm not the enemy, Jon."

Of course not, you're just being *sensitive*.

"I'm sorry Jon, we'll make it up to you."

What?

"Next season. What would you like to do? Any part you want."

I should have been offended. It was clearly a bribe. But it was a great bribe. Any part I wanted. And I am an actor. I like to work. So . . . I thought about it. Any part. I played Hamlet when I was younger, I've played Richard, I've played the Scots King, even Lear, but I'd never had a chance at . . .

Othello.

"What?"

Othello.

"Do you really think that's appropriate?"

Excuse me?

"People would think—it would just be insensitive, that's all."

Insensitive?

"Yes. You can't play Othello."

Why not?

And he stares at me for a moment like I'm some sort of idiot. "He's a black man."

I'm an actor. I play different roles, I inhabit different characters.

"But he's black."

So you're saying I don't have the skill to play Othello?

"No, I'm saying you don't have the pigmentation."

Does that mean that every actor who plays Shylock has to be circumcised? I've heard of actors doing a lot of things for a role, but I don't know.

"What about Iago? He has more lines anyway. You'd make a fabulous Iago."

I see . . . And your decision to cancel *Merchant* . . . it's final?

"It's my responsibility, Jonathan."

I think that's the only time since he hired me—the only time in ten years he has ever called me "Jonathan." Only my mother still calls me Jonathan.

"And you know Jonathan, when the shit hits the fan—"

It's your fan.

He nodded.

But it doesn't have to be. What if I meet with the protesters?

Talk to them?

He smiled, but it wasn't a happy smile. "They don't want to talk."

He was wrong. They were only too happy to talk. What they didn't want to do was listen.

The university had already issued an invitation. Professor Berman issued an invitation. To the company. To discuss.

Not a true invitation, really. More like an open letter in the newspaper. A dare.

I had no choice, really. I wasn't fighting for me. I wasn't fighting for a job. I'm still playing Prospero every second night. Good seats still available. No, I was fighting for Shakespeare. Fighting for art. And I went in there feeling like it was a holy war and I was on the side of the angels.

It started promisingly enough. There was no spitting. And the introduction was polite. They applauded when I stood up to speak. But that was the last friendly sound I heard. I tried to explain the history of the play, the context, the importance, but Professor Berman wasn't listening. Thinking back on it, I'm not certain anyone was.

"It's hurtful," she said.

Hurtful? But this is probably the best known Jew in fiction.

"Yes," she says. "Criminal isn't it?" Then she tells me that more Christians have heard of Shylock than Tevye. More Christians have heard of Shylock than Moses. That in Japan, China, Africa—the first Jew, perhaps the only Jew, they'll ever be exposed to is Shylock. And she tells me the history of *Merchant* is the history of anti-Semitism.

But it's not a history, I say. It's a play.

And she says that's her point. If it's just another play, why keep performing it?

I tried to say something about poetry, about humanity, about—but she wasn't listening. No one was listening. No, she had a story of her own. About her son. About how when he was in high school they were teaching *Merchant* and he was the only Jew in his class and for two years afterwards they called him Shylock. And some days, when he was walking home, they threw pennies at him.

I didn't know what to say to that. What do you say? Is it Shakespeare's fault? Is it the teacher? Is it—

And then she asks me—"Would you want your child to see this play?"

Actually, she has—and we had a wonderful discussion about it afterwards, about anti-Semitism and what it means to be Jewish. But I didn't get a chance to say that. I didn't get a chance to say anything.

"Where would war, any war, have been without the cartoon enemy? Where would the Holocaust have been without the cartoon Jew? If the Germans had seen Jews as human beings instead of . . . Shylocks."

So Shylock was responsible for the Holocaust?

Suddenly the room is alive with suggestions.

One girl—sorry, woman—says, "Why can't you just take out the word Jew and make him generic? You know, like make him a Christian or an atheist or something?"

Then another woman wants to know if we could just rewrite the play and remove Shylock altogether.

I say I'm not sure that would work too well.

I ask the class if they think this play could turn them into anti-Semites. No. None of the students believe it can affect them—but they are all certain it can affect "other people."

So Professor Berman asks if it worries me that the next time someone fire-bombs a synagogue or spray paints the tombstones at the Jewish cemetery they might be doing it with Shylock in mind. I said I couldn't imagine that happening. She said she can.

And then she tells me that Anthony Burgess, you know, the guy who wrote *Clockwork Orange*—if you don't know don't feel bad, she had to tell me, which made me feel even worse—he had always said art needed no defense other than that it was art. That stories weren't dangerous.

Then those two little boys in Britain beat another little boy to death using the kicks they'd learned watching *Mighty Morphin Power Rangers*. And Burgess recanted on his deathbed. He decided that maybe art was dangerous after all. That maybe he shouldn't have published *Clockwork Orange*.

I replied that to the best of my knowledge Shakespeare has never written an episode of *Mighty Morphin Power Rangers*. Although apparently Francis Bacon wrote a few.

(To whoever laughs) I'm glad you think it's funny. She didn't.

Apparently Burgess said writers were dangerous. That artists are dangerous. Words are dangerous.

So does that mean we lock up all the words?

I wish I'd said that the other day. I didn't.

I suggested tacking on a happy ending, a Tate ending, where Shylock refuses to convert and the court, seeing the error of their ways and sensing the awesome untapped nobility in this fine old man, gives him his money and his freedom. His daughter runs back into his loving arms and embraces him and Lorenzo declares that if it means keeping Jessica he's willing to risk the scorn of his Christian brethren by converting to Judaism to be with his one true love.

And one young woman says, "that could work." And the other students start to agree. They thought I was serious. They really did want Tate's *Romeo and Juliet* where everyone lives happily ever after. No more tragedy because tragedy requires an audience capable of drawing their own conclusions and God protect those who reach the wrong ones.

So she asks whether I'm a Jew or an actor. What was I supposed to say to that? I thought I was both. Fine, I'm not religious. I don't go to *shul* much, except on Yom Kippur, but does that mean I'm not a Jew?

Then she tells me: "You know that Hitler loved your play."

Now it was "my" play. And I was on the side of Hitler.

So I ask if she thinks *Merchant of Venice* should be banned.

She doesn't skip a beat. "I certainly see no positive reason for it being performed."

Why stop there? Why not just remove it from all the collected works and burn it?

There was a long silence. Everyone was quiet for a moment. This time I felt I had won. That Shakespeare had won. For a moment I believed they were truly ashamed.

"I don't think that would be practical," she says. And she smiled. I think she was kidding. But I'm not sure.

And then she asks again—why should anyone perform this play?

And then this boy pipes up, "How would you feel if the play was set in Israel instead of Venice and instead of a Jew, Shylock was a Palestinian? How would you feel about that?"

Then another student tells me that she's Jewish and she saw a production at Stratford—in Ontario—that was set in fascist Italy. And that she was much more "comfortable" with that production.

I said I was very happy for her but that we'd obviously chosen to interpret the play in a different way.

And she wanted to know why—why we couldn't have chosen an interpretation that would be more comfortable for Jews to watch.

And for a moment I'm wondering, maybe she's right. Maybe this is too negative.

But then I think—is that the goal now? To second guess everything we do? To make people comfortable?

Are we only allowed to do *Merchant* if we do a version that has the approval of the Jewish Congress?

Can we only produce *Taming of the Shrew* if the local Women's Shelter is on-side?

Does every production of every play have to be "comfortable" for everyone in the audience?

(To audience, genuinely asking.) Does it?

Is that what you want?

Then, before I can answer, another boy: "It's obvious you're a racist. Why don't you just admit you're a racist and that this is a racist play."

Racist?

I was so angry, so . . .

So I start explaining again how this is art and how it's a classic and . . . I don't know what I said after that. I don't think I made any more sense than Tony did.

I know how I ended it though. It's art, I said. Isn't that reason enough?

And Marcia T. Berman said, "That's like saying it's all right to burn a building as long as the fire is pretty."

And when I left the lecture hall I felt like I'd been spit on by a hundred people.

And while I'm walking to the car it hits me—why I'm so angry. At her. At these kids.

I hear "racist" and I see my father as a four-year-old boy in Odessa. The Cossacks are there. They've come to take my grandfather away. No one knows why. No one ever found out why. And my father—four years old—is holding tight to his father's legs. And one of the Cossacks turns to my grandmother and tells her that if her little boy—if my father—doesn't let go of his father's legs that they'll chop off his arms.

I hear racist and I wonder what happened to my grandfather. To my *zaida*.

This little shit hears racist and he sees Shakespeare.

You know, I suppose I should thank Marcia T. Berman. If she'd never spit at me I probably never would have thought about that. Or what it means to be Jewish. Mind you, without *Merchant* I'm not sure she would have thought about it either.

I know. I haven't behaved myself after all. And I haven't answered your questions. I'm sorry.

(*He takes off the last of the make-up.*)

I also thought about what she said about Burgess and I'll tell you what I wish I'd told her, what I wish I'd told that class. Maybe Burgess is right. Maybe it is all dangerous.

Galileo was dangerous. Moses was dangerous. Maybe Shakespeare is dangerous. Maybe that's a chance we've got to take. Maybe that's what art is.

And maybe you don't just do the play because it's art. Maybe you do it because it makes you talk about issues like this.

I did a bit of reading about Nazis and Shakespeare the other day. And she was right, Hitler was very fond of *The Merchant of Venice*. However, he wouldn't allow productions of *Othello*. He felt it was "offensive" because it showed a black man in a position of authority. Hitler was afraid it might give people the wrong idea.

And I suppose Professor Berman worries that our play will give you the wrong idea. That you are those "other people"—the ones who will watch *Merchant* and turn into a rampaging mob of crazed Klansmen screaming for the blood of your Jewish neighbours. Personally, I'd like to believe you're not that stupid. That people aren't that stupid. But if you are, then please, boo all you like.

SHYLOCK: What judgement shall I dread, doing no wrong?
    You have among you many a purchas'd slave
    Which, like your asses and your dogs and mules
    You use in abject and in slavish parts
    Because you bought them; shall I say to you
    "Let them be free, marry them to your heirs—
    Why sweat they under burdens?—Let their beds
    Be made as soft as yours, and let their palates
    Be seasoned with such viands?" You will answer

"The slaves are ours." So do I answer you:
The pound of flesh which I demand of him
Is dearly bought, 'tis mine, and I will have it.
If you deny me, fie upon your law!
There is no force in the decrees of Venice.
I stand for judgement; answer; shall I have it?

(He takes a bow, smiles, salutes and exits—proudly . . .)

The Unkindest Cuts of All

Shakespearean Censorship Through the Ages

Written and Compiled by Mark Leiren-Young
(additional research by Joan Watterson)

1597: *The Tragedie of King Richard the Second* becomes a bit less tragic when England's Queen Elizabeth orders publishers to remove the scene where the King is deposed. The scene vanishes from productions and published scripts until after the Queen's death in 1603.

1600: Jack Cade, the rebel leader in *Henry IV*, is a little too rebellious for the age and the script is selectively edited to remove lines that might provoke too much negative sentiment towards the monarchy. However, censors appeared to have no problem with Cade's line, "The first thing we do, let's kill all the lawyers." The play remains out of print from 1600 to 1619.

1606: England passes a Parliamentary "Acte to Restraine

Abuses of Players." The Puritans begin to purify Shakespeare as the Master of Revels oversees the removal of offensive or profane language and words like "God," "heaven" and "zounds" (a slang reference to Christ's wounds) are temporarily vanquished to purgatory. The ever-talkative, and profane, Sir John Falstaff suddenly finds himself at a loss for words.

1640: William Sankey gets the Vatican's blessing to produce a more Catholic Shakespeare. *Measure for Measure*, with it's mockery of friars and nuns, doesn't measure up and is left out of his collection as are lines like the Clown's joke in *All's Well that Ends Well* referring to an answer being as fit "as the nun's lips to the friar's mouth."

1642: Cromwell declares theatre immoral and drama becomes illegal in England. The theatres are closed but opera houses are allowed to remain open. The fact that operas are making more money at the time is undoubtedly a coincidence.

1660: Charles the Second returns to the throne and theatres are re-opened. However, unlike some British Royals, they are supposed to be kept "chaste." William Davenant, manager of one of London's two legally licensed theatres gets the exclusive rights to produce nine of Shakespeare's plays and makes sure he doesn't risk losing those rights by offending the royal patrons. Macbeth's speech to a servant, "The devil damn thee black, thou cream-faced loon! Where gott'st thou that goose look?" is chastened into "No Friend, what means thy change of Countenance?"

1681: Nahum Tate rewrites various tragedies including *King Lear* to provide happy endings—Cordelia marries Edgar and the two live happily ever after. It's a hit and the Hollywood ending is born.

1692: Thomas Rymer complains in his pamphlet, *A Short View of Tragedy* about the dangers of *Othello*. He is upset that Desdemona does not conduct herself as proper nobility, Iago fails to fulfill his duties as a soldier and Shakespeare has allowed a black man to marry a white woman and rise to such a position of power. Writes Rymer: "With us a Black-amoor might rise to be a Trumpeter; but Shakespear would not have him less than a Lieutenant-General. With us a Moor might marry some little drab, or Small-coal Wench; Shakespear, would provide him the Daughter and Heir of some Great Lord, or Privy-Councellor: And all the town should reckon it a very suitable match."

1772: *Othello* debuts in France and after "several of the prettiest women in Paris fainted in the most conspicuous boxes, and were publicly carried out of the house" the translator, Ducis rewrote the ending with Brabantio racing in to save Desdemona just as the dagger is raised. In case you're wondering why this is a dagger you see before you, Ducis had already decided a pillow was too cruel. The play was published with both endings but Talma, the actor playing Othello, disapproved of the heroic rescue and one night re-established Shakespeare's ending by ignoring the script and killing Desdemona.

1773: Back in Britain Francis Gentleman edits Bell's edition of

plays "as acted" at the Theatre Royal. The merry Gentleman's version sanitizes *Othello* cleaning up references to
witchcraft and sexuality. "Would you, the supervisor,
grossly gape on? Behold her topped?" is presented topless,
ending at "behold her." He apologizes for retaining certain
of Iago's more explicit sexual references about catching
Desdemona and Cassio declaring, "We wish the greater
part of his speech were omitted. Nothing material would
be lost and delicacy would be better sustained." In most
texts delicacy prevailed and words like "whore," "cuck-
old," "strumpet" and "top" disappeared—leaving Othello
to be provoked into a murderous rage at the thought of his
wife playing Scrabble with another man. On the sophisti-
cated continent, France's Voltaire revolted against *Othello*
as well, translating and correcting some of Shakespeare's
more suggestive passages.

1788: *King Lear* cuts too close to home while the mad King
George III occupies the throne and the play disappears
from the British stage until George's abdication.

1807: Henrietta Bowdler sits down to start crossing out all the
dirty words, blasphemous passages and lewd references in
Shakespeare's repertoire. Surprisingly there were still
enough words left to allow for the publication of *The
Family Shakespeare.* No editor was named because, as is
explained in the text "Shakespeare's words were simply
too potent to be trusted with a lady," so it would have been
improper for a proper lady like Henrietta to understand the
references that she was excising. When the book is reprinted in 1818 the official credit is given to her brother, Dr.

Thomas Bowdler and The English language gains the word "Bowdlerize" in exchange for Shakespeare's plays losing their sense of humour and roughly ten percent of their content. Thomas Bowdler is so delighted with his newfound fame that he goes on to produce a family version of that notoriously racy book, Gibbon's *The Decline and Fall of the Roman Empire*. Ironically, Henrietta's role is censored and her contribution to literary history isn't discovered until 1966.

1822: Knock knock jokes. The Bowdler Shakespeare is such a hit that others try their hand at sanitizing the Bard. Rev. J.R. Pitman releases *School-Shakespeare* and in true used car dealer fashion he decides that everything must go. Where the Bowdlers had managed to reduce the famous drunken Porter scene in *Macbeth* from 20 to 14 lines by removing references to Hell, Pitman tidies it up even further by removing any indications that this is a drunken rant. Pitman's pithy version of it simply reads: "Here's a knocking indeed! Knock, knock, knock. Anon, anon; I pray you, remember the porter." With a memorable monologue like that, who could possibly forget him?

1849: An American Bowdler is born. Professor John W.S. Hows decides to clean up Shakespeare, American style. *Romeo and Juliet* is socially corrected when Juliet suddenly becomes 18, Falstaff takes leave of *Henry IV,* Part One and *Othello* is "improved" by ending the play after Act Three.

1858: Shakespeare in Wonderland. Lewis Carroll starts to write *The Girl's Own Shakespeare* complaining that existing editions of the Bard's texts, "are not sufficiently expurgated." Fortunately, he is distracted by a large white rabbit and his project is never completed.

1865: Thomas Bullfinch of Boston, Mass. cleans up *Macbeth* texts with a bit of that damned spot remover. His book *Shakespeare Adapted for Reading Classes and the Family Circle* has Lady Macbeth examining her hand and proclaiming, "Out crimson spot. Out, I say." Other spots in the plays also vanish. Meanwhile, the Germans decide Shakespeare needs more happy endings and popular editions appear where comic characters like the gravediggers vanish from *Hamlet* and Juliet wakes up just in time to save Romeo.

1931: An ounce of prevention is worth a pound of flesh. At the request of Jewish organizations, *The Merchant of Venice* is removed from the high school curriculum in Buffalo and Manchester, New York.

1934: *Coriolanus* is french fried when the government of France bans the production and then the script itself because its politics were seen as unflattering to the government.

1936: Shakespeare is put "on trial" in Palestine. Director Leopold Jessner stages *The Merchant of Venice* at the Habimah Theatre (which eventually becomes the National Theatre of Israel) and, according to John Gross in his book, *Shylock, A Legend and its Legacy*, "the author, the director and the theatre were all arraigned."

1939: After all foreign dramatists are banned from Germany, Hitler personally intervenes to save Shakespeare. *The Merchant of Venice* is a big hit during the Nazi reign, although there are concerns about the issue of intermarriage and the play is sometimes altered so that Shylock's daughter Jessica is illegitimate and able to marry a proper citizen. Gross notes that some of Shakespeare's plays were censored in Nazi Germany. *Othello*, for example, was banned on "racial grounds" (although the play was often "fixed" by making Othello an Arab) and *Antony and Cleopatra* was attacked because it was "too perverse and effeminate" and showed a man putting a woman above his country. Meanwhile, Joe Stalin becomes the Soviet Union's top theatre critic, and *Hamlet* is banned until his death in 1953 because he doesn't like the theme of regicide.

1941: German propaganda minister Joseph Goebbels becomes his country's defacto artistic director and any Shakespeare production suddenly requires his approval.

1946: American authorities ban productions of *Coriolanus* from occupied Germany because of its political and military themes.

1949: Got to pick a pocket or two . . . (Rosenberg v. Board of Education) Jewish parents in Brooklyn, New York sued the Board of Education claiming that their children's right to an education free of religious bias was violated by portrayals of Jews in both *Oliver Twist* and Shakespeare's *The Merchant of Venice*. The King's County Supreme Court ruled that the

Board: ". . . acted in good faith without malice or prejudice and in the best interests of the school system entrusted to their care and control." and added: "Except where a book has been maliciously written for the apparent purpose of fomenting a bigoted and intolerant hatred against a particular racial or religious group, public interest in a free and democratic society does not warrant or encourage the suppression of any book . . ."

1955: Beam me up Bard. William Shatner and Lorne Greene star in *The Merchant of Venice* at Canada's Stratford Festival. The production is condemned as anti-Semitic by the *Canadian Jewish News*.

1965: The Gang of Four adds a fifth conspirator when Shakespeare is declared counter-revolutionary and his plays are banned from China as part of Mao's Cultural Revolution. The ban is not revoked until 1977.

1975: Yo, Ophelia. To make Shakespeare more user-friendly for Americans, a new edition of Shakespeare updates the language so, "O, what a rogue and peasant slave am I." becomes "Oh, what a bum and miserable flunky I am."

1980: *The Merchant of Venice* is removed from the curriculum in Midland, Michigan because of concerns that teaching children about the Jewish character of Shylock is just not kosher.

1980: A rose by any other name? The new Harcourt Brace Janovich edition of *Romeo and Juliet* "omits" approximately 10 percent of the script which is dismissed as "trivial or ribald wordplay and especially difficult static passages of poetry."

1981: It's time to change the channel. When the PBS affiliate in New York announces the broadcast date for the BBC's production of *The Merchant of Venice* the station receives letters of protest from the Anti-Defamation League of the B'Nai Brith and the Executive Committee of the Committee to Bring Nazi War Criminals to Justice in the USA.

1985: Kosher kiwi? The English Club at New Zealand's Victoria University decides they will not show the film of *The Merchant of Venice,* explaining: "The play remains available for serious study but need not be displayed to the idly curious."

1986: Is this a censor I see before me? *Macbeth* is too scary for some students in Colorado when parents challenge it as required reading because of the emphasis on, "death, suicide, ghosts and Satan."

1987: To show or not to show? The government of Nepal refuses to allow the production of a Nepali version of *Hamlet* because it could offend Royalist sensibilities. According to the Toronto *Globe and Mail*, Nepalese officials had previously rejected requests to perform *Macbeth* and *Hamlet* "on grounds both plays offended Nepal's royal tradition."

1988: In an essay entitled "Abusive Amusement," Susan Cole

discusses watching the Stratford, Ontario production of "Shakespeare's ode to female oppression," *The Taming of the Shrew,* and wondering about "the thorny problem of whether major theatre companies ought to bother with revivals of obnoxiously unenlightened works." Cole notes that, "many feminists have insisted that *The Taming of the Shrew* should be shredded and never presented on our national stages."

1989: Not to be. According to the *Boston Globe, Hamlet* is banned from an Israeli detention camp because of Hamlet's musings about whether it's better to take up arms or suffer in silence. Shalom.

1990: "When shall we three meet again?" It won't be in a school library if some Christian groups have their way. The American Library Association reports that the most popular reason for removing books from school libraries is their inclusion of supernatural events. Among the plays that have disappeared from some American libraries: *Hamlet, Macbeth, The Tempest* and *A Midsummer Night's Dream.*

1993: Time for Romeo to grow up. The Canadian government passes a law outlawing child pornography, which prohibits the depiction of anyone who is—or appears to be—under the age of 18 in a sexual context. Sandra Bernstein, in her on-line history of Canadian censorship, notes that: "The law is so broad that critics, all of whom support restrictions on genuine child pornography, argue that many coming-of-age movies, including *Romeo and Juliet* . . . could not have been made had the law been in effect at the time."

1994: The Artistic Director of Canada's Stratford Festival indicates that perhaps his festival won't be bothering with "revivals of obnoxiously unenlightened works." At a public forum Richard Monette announces that *The Merchant of Venice* and *The Taming of the Shrew* will not be performed this season because of concerns that the plays are offensive. Monette says he hasn't been a fan of *Merchant* since appearing in a Stratford production where he was disturbed by the audience's obvious hatred of Shylock and explains that, "Half the women on my staff and on the board of directors said they could not possibly support" the staging of *Shrew*. Meanwhile, Jane Brown, a school teacher in London, England sparks a furore by refusing to take her class to a ballet production of *Romeo and Juliet* because it is "blatantly heterosexual."

1995: *Twelfth Night* is removed from the school curriculum in Merrimack, New Hampshire because it violates a policy that bans any instruction or education which could be seen to be "encouraging or supporting homosexuality as a positive lifestyle alternative." The board is concerned because the play includes scenes of a young woman disguising herself as a boy. Apparently, school board officials are now on the lookout for a blatantly heterosexual ballet.

1997: Too much Shakespeare? Acclaimed drama professor Jared Sakren—former teacher of Annette Bening, Val Kilmer and Frances McDormand—is fired by Arizona State University for teaching too many musty old "classics" and neglecting such modern classics as, um, *Betty the Yeti*. A real life *Comedy of Errors*, Sakren successfully sued for wrongful dismissal and received a settlement of $395,000 U.S.

1998: Kill all the lawyers? A school teacher in Loudon County, Virginia had her production of *Twelfth Night* slashed from the schedule because of a ban on weapons—even looka-like weapons—from schools.

2001: *Merchant* becomes anti-Islamic? Canada's Stratford festi-val redirects their production of *Merchant* after complaints that their portrayal of the King of Morocco is a racial stereo-type. Meanwhile, in Gauteng, South Africa a committee of teachers responsible for monitoring the curriculum recom-mends banning Shakespeare's plays because *Julius Caesar* is sexist; *Antony and Cleopatra* is undemocratic and racist; *King Lear* is boring and *Hamlet* is depressing.

This is by no means a complete listing of all the times The Bard has been censored, banned or Bowdlerized. Noel Perrin writes in his book, *Dr. Bowdler's Legacy*, "Shakespeare's plays have been bowdlerized at least a hundred separate times and *Gulliver's Travels* almost as often. At the end of the nineteenth century, even a poet as austere as Milton sometimes appeared in school texts "with necessary omissions," designed to shield excitable teenagers from the knowledge that Satan committed incest, or from the realization that Eve had a good figure, or just from the knowledge that she and Adam did not, in their garden years, wear anything to bed. Even if I wanted to give a list of all the expurgations there have been, I would be prevented by lack of information. I know of perhaps three thousand British and American expurgations, but there are undoubtedly thousands more that I don't know about."

Anyone with more information on these, or other incidents related to the censorship of Shakespeare's texts, is invited to relay them to the publisher or to contact the author via e.mail (mark@leiren-young.ca) so that this timeline will be more comprehensive the next time this book is reprinted.

Oraf

Mark Leiren-Young is a Canadian playwright, screen-writer and journalist. As a playwright he's best known for his controversial dramas (including *Shylock, Basically Good Kids* and *Dim Sum Diaries*) and political and social satires (including dozens of topical revues with his comedy duo, Local Anxiety). Mark's plays have been produced at theatres across Canada and have also been staged in the U.S. and Australia. Mark's television writing credits include episodes of *Ace Lightning, Toy Castle, Mentors, Psi Factor, Stickin' Around, ReBoot, Grand Illusions*, CBC's *Life and Times* and the award-winning TV special, *Greenpieces—An Eco-Comedy*, which he also co-produced and co-starred in. As a journalist, Mark has written for *Time, Maclean's, The Utne Reader* and dozens of other news-papers and magazines. He is co-author of *The Little Book of Reform* and has released two CDs with Local Anxiety, *Forgive Us, We're Canadian* and *Greenpieces*. Mark's most recent play, *Articles of Faith*, dealing with the Anglican Church's ongoing debate over the blessing of same-sex unions, premiered earlier this year. He currently lives in Toronto.